200 Years of Carolina House Trust

(formerly Dundee Royal Orphan Institution)

"Plenty to eat and braw claes"

By Wendy Glass
Design by Stuart Cameron @ design1OO

Acknowledgements

Dawn Anderson, Bill Black, Andy Chalmers, Bill Chalmers, Bill Christie, Central Library Local History Department, Stephen Clark, DC Thomson Archives, Dundee City Archives, Friends of Dundee City Archives, Leah Henderson, Les Lumb, Angie MacDonald, Brenda E. McGilliard, Calum McKenzie, Vikki Merrilees, Michelle, Doug Millar, Bill Pollock, Lauren Reeves, Doug Thomson, Murray Thomson, Heather White, Jerry Wright

Credits

Many thanks to DC Thomson & Co Ltd, Dundee's Art Galleries and Museums and Dundee City Archives for the use of their photographs and images.

The printing of this book has been generously subsidised by Northwood Charitable Trust and The Logan Charitable Trust, courtesy of Miss JL Thomson.

Published by Carolina House Trust
Printed by Winter & Simpson Print, Dundee
Copyright Wendy Glass / Carolina House Trust
ISDN 9780993333804

Foreword

It gives me great pleasure to write this foreword for the short history of Carolina House Trust - formally Dundee Royal Orphan Institution - marking our first 200 years.

The bicentenary is an ideal opportunity to thoroughly research the rich history of a Dundee institution and to tell the true story of Carolina House Trust. However, although our bicentenary is the impetus to record our history, it is not the only factor. This is a time of constant change for children and young people, and interpreting our past is a key part of thinking about our future.

Our rich and eventful past cannot be separated from the mixed fortunes of one of Scotland's iconic industrialised cities. Factual records and accounts have been woven with historic and personal stories to provide a chronological account of the local people behind the establishment of Dundee Royal Orphan Institution in 1815 through to the present day.

Above all, our bicentenary should remind us that Carolina House Trust is about people. As with all history, most of what we have is based on fragments of the past and to make a coherent story, both contemporary material and conjecture play a part. The fascinating historic details add colour and greater understanding to the accounts of children, young people, parents, staff and directors over 200 years of one of Scotland's oldest children's charities.

Our adventures into the past have highlighted how much we owe to the chroniclers of the Trust's history, and the enthusiastic stewards and custodians of our legacy today. The first outing to Dundee City Archives revealed a treasure trove of information. Dundee's journalistic past revealed many reports of the Orphanage and the material held by DC Thomson's Archives helped with the recent past, as well as much older source material. The team at The McManus, Dundee's Art Gallery & Museum, have also been incredibly helpful.

The history of Dundee Royal Orphan Institution reflects the social and economic ups and downs of Dundee. Bonnie it is not in places but the Institution's faith and belief in helping children for the last 200 years is unquestionable.

Acting Director of Operations,
Carolina House Trust

19th century Dundee

Chapter 1

The Foundations of Carolina House

At 10am on September 18, 1815, nine boys and 12 girls became the first residents of Dundee Orphan Institution – and 200 years later, Carolina House Trust, as the charity has been known since 1961, continues to provide support to children and young people who are in care or who have left care.

The 21 orphans who filed into the Orphanage in Paradise Road were in desperate need. In the early 19th century, life was grim for the poor and destitute of Scotland's newly-industrialised cities, especially children without parents or whose parents were unable to look after them.

In those days, orphans were cared for by the Parish and arrangements would often be made for orphans to be boarded out, perhaps with a local family or a farmer looking for extra manpower. "The children are rescued from pauperism, forget their old haunts, evil parents and the poorhouse," reported a 19th century Poor Law Inspector, commenting on the practice of sending orphaned pauper children to live in the country.

However, although this system worked relatively well when people remained in or near the Parish where they were born, as more families moved into Dundee in search of work in the city's textile industry, it became increasingly difficult for the local parish church to cope with the high numbers of orphans and, as described in the records of the time, 'fatherless children'.

There were jobs to be found in Dundee but life in the city was hard. Cramped housing, a meagre diet, long hours, poor working conditions and very little sanitation all took their toll on the city's workers – and for those who were unable to find work, life was incredibly difficult.

Life expectancy rates in Dundee were much lower than in the nearby countryside, resulting in large numbers of families with only one parent – or none. For these children, there was little hope other than life on the streets or a bed in the Poorhouse.

On February 9, 1815, John Whittet junior, William Dick, David Adams (who would later become Dundee Orphan Institution's first master) and George Scott met in the Baker's Room of the Trades Hall in Dundee to 'deliberate on the propriety of attempting to open an orphan establishment in Dundee.'

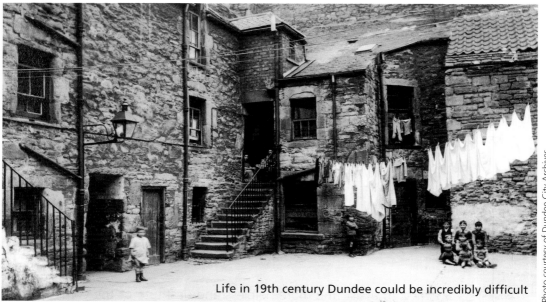

Life in 19th century Dundee could be incredibly difficult

Photo courtesy of Dundee City Archives

As a result of this meeting, one month later, a group of forward-thinking Dundonians – doctors, mill owners, ministers, merchants, estate owners, the Dundee Provost (and several of their wives) – met to further discuss establishing an institution to care for and educate the city's growing number of orphans.

A Board of Directors was appointed and ground work began. Funds had to be raised, a suitable building found, staff appointed…

As plans were made, the loss of 17 lives in the 1815 Tay Ferry Disaster on May 28 brought tragedy to the city – and, according to a newspaper report: 'A good many people were ready to show their sympathy in practical form.' A meeting was held in the Steeple Church just ten days later to establish, organise and raise funds for Dundee's new orphanage, and to make arrangements so people could donate 'bedding etc'.

For many years, the immense public support for the Orphanage in the wake of the Tay Ferry Disaster led to this tragedy being credited as the reason for the founding of the Dundee Orphan Institution. However, a few years ago, Jerry Wright, a member of the Friends of Dundee City Archives, discovered that the Tay Ferry Disaster actually occurred several months after the founding of the Dundee Orphan Institution.

"The added publicity worked to the Directors' advantage," reported Jerry, who also discovered that those concerned in raising funds for the Orphanage were quick to capitalise on the increased public awareness of the plight of orphaned children.

Donations flooded in and, according to reports of the time, once the sum of £700 had been raised, 'Mr Black's House' in Dundee's Paradise Road was rented for the sum of £20 per annum, a 'kindly woman' was installed as matron, two teachers were recruited and Dundee Orphan Institution opened its doors.

The Founders

Dundee Orphan Institution was founded in 1815 by The Dundee Society for Educating Orphans, Fatherless Children and the Children of the Industrious Poor, and is one of the oldest children's charities in Scotland.

The Society aimed to assist 'the more helpless and destitute of the community – orphans and fatherless children', while also striving to educate children whose parents worked in Dundee's textile mills, as well as in the city's shipyards and whaling industry.

Although the Society's Directors were all men, women played a significant part in the committee which managed the charity and the Orphanage, which was very unusual at the time. A board of Lady Governesses was elected, mainly wives of the Directors, who acted as assistants to the Society's Patroness, Mrs Alexander Pitcairn.

1815 Directors

- John Baxter
- David Blair junior
- Peter Brown
- William Dick (surgeon)
- James Erskine
  Esq of Linlathen (Patron)
- George Gray
- Provost John Guild
- Rev H Horsley

- David Jobson junior
- Robert Jobson
- James J Johnston
- William Lindsay
- Hugh McKay
- Rev Dr McLauchlan
- James Montgomery
- William Neish
- Rev Dr Nicoll

- Rev Dr Peters
- Alexander Pitcairn
- RS Rintoul
- Captain Scott
- George Scott
- Adam Tait
- Robert Thornton
- William Urquhart

Other Notable Early Directors

William Edward Baxter. Grandson of William Baxter, the founder of Baxter Brothers textile business. Businessman, travel writer and Liberal MP for Montrose 1855-1885.

James Chalmers. Bookseller, printer, newspaper publisher and inventor of the adhesive postage stamp.

Thomas Neish. Dundee merchant, often credited with starting the Dundee jute industry.

William Gardiner. Umbrella maker and botanist – several of his plant collections can be found at Kew Gardens and other botanical gardens throughout the UK.

George Duncan (Chair of the Board, 1846). MP for Dundee 1841-1857, director of several shipping and insurance companies and a dedicated philanthropist. After retiring from public life in 1857, George Duncan lived in seclusion at his mansion in Dundee's Magdelene Green, The Vine.

The Right Honourable Lord Panmure (President of the Board, 1846). Landowner, MP for Forfarshire 1796-1831 and patron of the arts, William Maule, 1st Baron Panmure, was born William Ramsay but changed his name to William Maule when he inherited Panmure Estate from his great uncle.

The Right Honourable Earl of Airlie (Vice President of the Board, 1846). Sir John Ogilvy of Inverquharity was MP for Dundee for 16 years and known as a generous benefactor. Instrumental in the establishment of Dundee Royal Infirmary and the Baldovan Insititute (Strathmartine Hospital), which cared for 'helpless and afflicted patients'.

6

Chapter 2

The First Dundee Orphan Institution

Despite the tragedy on the river, and local legend, of the 21 children admitted to Dundee Orphan Institution at 10am on September 18, 1815, only four appear to have been linked to the ferry boat sinking in the Tay.

Stewart Smith (10) and Betty Smith (11) shared their surname with one of the men who drowned, while Janet Luke (10) and Jean Luke (7) are thought to have been the daughters of John Luke, a flaxdresser who drowned with two of his other children.

However, there are several unconfirmed accounts that all but one of the children who were admitted had been left fatherless following the Tay Ferry Disaster, while a Dundee Royal Orphan Institution booklet from the 1950s mentions how five young children who had already lost their parents, were left without anyone to care for them after their older brother, 'Young John Bennett', drowned in the Tay Ferry Disaster.

"Now he was gone, what was to become of these five helpless children and of the three others left destitute?" the booklet relates. "The answer was not long in coming – a house was found big enough to accommodate all the children so that members of a family need not be separated from each other."

Perhaps the most notable of the Orphanage's first residents was Bell McCole, the ten-year-old daughter of a Dundee soldier killed at the Battle of Waterloo in June, 1815. Before she was admitted to the Orphanage, Bell had been staying with Isabel Hayton at Scouring Burn – close to Verdant Works jute mill. When it was announced that

One of the narrow Dundee streets where many of the city's workers lived

places were available at the Orphanage, Bell and her guardian, along with the other children under consideration for a place at the Orphanage, attended the 'inspection' of potential residents by seven of the Directors.

Bell and 20 other orphans must have passed the test as they were offered places at Dundee Orphan Institution and the chance to escape a future that, until then, must have looked very bleak indeed.

Conditions at Dundee Orphan Institution were basic but the Society's Minute Books, which are held by The City of Dundee Archives, reveal that there was considerable emphasis on ensuring ample supplies of bedding, provisions, clothing, school books and bibles. To fund the day-to-day expenses of the Orphanage, contribution boxes were placed in banks, coffee rooms and inns throughout the city, fundraising events such as theatre performances were held and the Institution also benefitted from donations from local philanthropists.

The Minute Books also report that the Master and the Mistress of the Orphanage – Mr David Adams and Miss Magdelene Moncur - were given very strict instructions that: 'The rod should be used as sparingly as possible on the boys and on no account to be used on the girls.'

The First Orphans

Boys:

McLachlan Low (9), Hill; Stewart Smith (10), Bottlework; John Brough (10), The Shore; James Evans (9), Murraygate; James Hobart (7), Perth Road; George Cargill (7), Cowgate; John Wilson (9), Pleasance; John McReddie (6), Scouring Burn; James Reid (9), Perth Road

Girls:

Elizabeth Weir (9), Seagate; Janet Luke (10), Hawkhill; Jean Luke (7), Seagate; Janet Young (10), Murraygate; Cath Mitchell (10), Scouring Burn; Mary Ann Buchanan (9), Hill; Bell McCole (10), Scouring Burn; Betty Tosh (16), Pleasance; Betty Smith (11), Bottlework; Betty Brough (10), Shore; Sarah Mudie (12), Murraygate; Betty Wilson (12), Pleasance

Wanted For The Dundee Orphan Institution

A TEACHER, well qualified to teach English grammatically, Writing, and Arithmetic.

The time of attendance as follows. Between eight and nine in the morning, from ten to twelve forenoon, from two to five in the afternoon, and from eight to nine in the evening. Sabbath attendance – an hour in the morning, and from six to eight if required. He must attend church with the children, if required, and act as Secretary to the Society.

Salary 80/- per annum, one year certain, and as much longer as the Institution shall flourish and the teacher shall continue to give satisfaction.

Applications, addressed to David Adams, Secretary to the Institution, any time prior to 15th August, will be carefully attended to.

NB None need apply but persons of character and abilities

Advertisement which appeared in Dundee, Perth & Cupar Advertiser, July 21, 1815

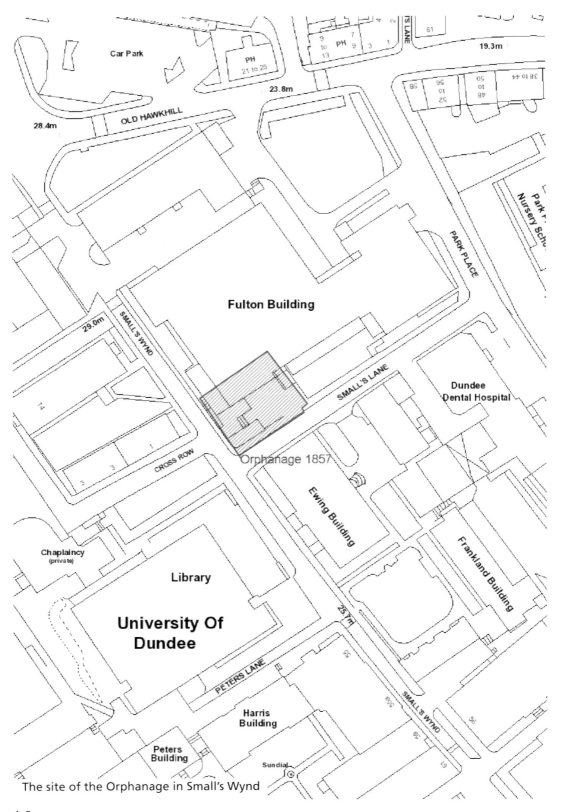

The site of the Orphanage in Small's Wynd

Chapter 3

Small's Wynd 1818 - 1870

The house in Paradise Road soon proved too small for the needs of the Orphanage so, when a larger property in Small's Wynd came onto the market, the Society's Directors agreed to buy it, with payment by monthly instalments.

Three years later, the Orphanage moved to Small's Wynd, enabling more of Dundee's ever-increasing population of orphans to be given a home. To help pay for the increased costs of the new, bigger building, the decision was made to admit day scholars, which also fulfilled one of the original aims of Dundee Orphan Institution to 'Educate the children of the industrious poor, who are unable to provide for the education of their families.'

For the sum of one shilling a quarter, children were educated alongside the orphans at Small's Wynd but the local economy had been hit by a slump in the textile trade, which had affected fundraising – and increased pressure on the Orphanage. The Orphanage was struggling to pay its bills and even successful appeals for donations to The Nine Incorporated Trades of Dundee, The Three United Trades, The Maltmen Fraternity, The Guildry and The Society of Writers failed to keep their debtors happy.

Initially, Orphanage Sundays had helped to keep the coffers solvent. At these annual services, two of the Orphanage's Directors and the Town Officer would stand at the door of the church. Following a heart-rending sermon about the plight of destitute children by a 'notable' minister or priest, they would collect donations as the congregations left. However, this was not enough to compensate for ever-rising costs and dwindling donations.

In addition, the reputation of the Orphanage had recently taken a blow thanks to the antics of a group of orphan boys. According to the Directors' Minutes of spring 1817, six boys had been caught entering a neighbouring garden in darkness and, after being 'chastised', had run away.

The next night, a further six boys ran away and when all 12 were caught and returned to the Orphanage, 'Mr Adam requested full power to chastise them as he felt appropriate, one of the ringleaders to be whipped and dismissed, the others admitted their part and getting a flogging with a tawse.'

Green Market

One month later, seven boys admitted breaking into a Poor Box and were expelled, while on Hallowe'en 1818, a group of boys 'absconded the house'. As a result, the Directors' Meetings Minutes of 1818 report that 'the boys were suitably exhorted and a punishment appointed to them of eight days privation of their usual play and a slight diminution of the usual allowance of food.'

This chain of events was disastrous for a charity which relied on public support and at the next meeting of the Directors, it was agreed that boys should no longer be accepted to the Orphanage. 'The committee were convinced that measure should likewise be taken to remove from the minds of the public the unfavourable impressions which have been created against the institution,' reported the Minutes, showing that, even 200 years ago, image was king.

James Chalmers & James Keillor

Amongst the first supporters of the Dundee Orphanage Society were none other than James Chalmers of adhesive postage stamp fame and James Keillor, whose business gave the world Dundee Marmalade.

In fact, it was James Chalmers who overturned the brief ban on boys being admitted to the orphanages, while there is a report in the January 23, 1819 Minutes that 'Mr Keillor, Confectioner, applied to the Directors for one of the orphan girls as an apprentice, which was agreed to.'

The 'No Boys' ruling was soon overturned – but the damage had been done and donations to the Orphanage continued to decrease.

By 1819, the Orphanage was in the middle of its first financial crisis – and it couldn't have happened at a worse time. Typhus Fever, dysentery, cholera and smallpox were endemic - Dundee was a very unhealthy place to live.

A Statistical Account of the period blamed the city's disastrous health record 'Either on account of the exhalations arising from the silt which is uncovered twice a day by the recess of the tide or from the original swampiness on which a considerable part of the town stands or from the impurity of the atmosphere from the smoke of steam engines used in manufactories or from the denseness of the population in many districts or from the negligent habits of the people as to cleanliness, or from a combination of several of these causes.'

But no matter what was taking its toll on the health of the city, the end result was the same - more destitute children on the streets of Dundee and higher costs for the Orphanage that was attempting to care for as many of them as possible.

A demand for £108 in unpaid arrears for the Small's Wynd building led to the discovery that there was only £43 in the Orphanage's bank account. Fundraising efforts were immediately increased but, although a ball organised by the Lady Governesses helped to pay this debt, it wasn't until a £1,000 legacy was received from a Mrs Lowden who lived in Hawkhill that the Directors could once again be confident about the future of the Orphanage. To ensure such a situation did not occur again, a range of stringent economy measures were introduced, including a limit of 15lbs of beef a week, the replacement of wheat & oat bread with oat & pease bread, a drastic reduction in the numbers of orphans and day scholars and staff wage cuts.

This final measure did not go down well with the Master of the Orphanage, Mr Adams, who was one of the original founders of the Society and had recently been given a substantial pay rise. He refused to accept his decreased salary and in August, 1821, was replaced by a married couple, Mr and Mrs Borland from New Rattray, who were paid £50 per annum, three quarters of the amount Mr Adams was paid every year.

On March 23, 1830, Dundee Orphan Institution was granted a Royal Charter by King George IV – and promptly assumed the title of Dundee Royal Orphan Institution. This appears to have boosted finances as, by 1833, the Orphanage had assets of £3,154. The Directors' Report that year noted that the cost of maintaining an orphan was 'about £6' a year, with a total of £30 having been spent on clothing and shoes, £73 on 'groceries and herring' and £6 for gas fitting and gas.

The same report provides a glimpse of what life must have been like for the orphans, describing how they 'benefitted from education; with considerable emphasis on Christian Religion, teaching in Reading, English Grammar, Writing and Arithmetic; female day pupils learned needlework, knitting and other useful domestic arts; female boarders did household work'.

Education, regular church-going and daily worship were considered very important but there were definite limits to how much the orphans and day pupils were taught. 'Although it is very desirable to give a liberal education to the rising generation, the Orphanage should be considered as much an asylum for the destitute as a seminary for educating youth…' declared one of the early Directors. 'To make the poor orphans good servants is of greater value than making them superior scholars.'

In fact, when a group of girls were caught 'fibbing', their punishment was 'to be taught to spin household yarn' on one of two spinning wheels bought specifically for this purpose.

By 1836, the Orphanage was facing another financial crisis. Donations from wealthy benefactors had dropped due to a slump in the textile and shipping industries, the now annual ball was running at a loss and Orphanage Sundays were proving much less successful as few people had a penny to spare. However, this time, the Directors decided to invest the meagre savings they had in Dundee's building industry, which proved, in the long term, to be a wise move.

Dundee's Nethergate running eastwards into the High Street

By 1844, a new Master and Matron were in charge at the Orphanage – Mr and Mrs Guild. However, due to continued financial restrictions, the number of orphans being cared for had been reduced to 17, with 45 day scholars. A plea for more subscriptions, an upturn in trade and a healthy return on the Orphanage's investments helped bring finances back under control. By 1857, there were 31 orphans residing there and following a Directors' Report that commented on the accommodation being substandard, the Small's Wynd Orphanage was extended.

However, the premises were still too cramped and, following a special appeal to the people of Dundee, £6,000 was raised, a site on Broughty Ferry Road was purchased and Broughty Ferry architect William Chalmers was commissioned to design a grand new building for Dundee Royal Orphan Institution.

Small's Wynd – House Contents August 25, 1821

•Bedding
14 beds full of chaff, 3 straw mattresses, 2 hair mattresses, 1 feather bolster, 3 feather pillows, 2 tick pillows, 36 pairs of sheets and 1 single, 2 pairs of Scotch and binder, 6 pairs of new sheets, 2 pairs of English blankets and binder for each of the girl's beds, 8 single English, 3 pairs of old Scotch, 10 pillowcases, 3 osnaburgh bags, 4 English blankets and 1 binder for Master's bed, 4 bolster cases, 6 course cases, 1 English for servant's bed, 2 pairs of Scotch and 1 binder for each of boy's beds, 4 pairs double, 3 pairs of new Scotch for store.

•Misc
20 caps, 15 tins, 3 lamps, 5 tubs, 3 tureens, 31 spoons, 2 screens, 2 small tubs, 2 boilers, 3 goblets, 1 flagon.

•Furniture, Provisions and Books
12 bolls meal, 1 live pigg, 8 bolls coals, 2 meal girnals, 1 meal barrel, 1 bauk and scales, 1 small kitt, 2 clothes screens, 2 spinning wheels, 1 reel, 1 bock, 1 greybeard for oil, 2 stoves for schoolrooms, 1 dozen ladles, 2 hall tables, 2 stones dressed flax, 1 knife box, 1 watering pan, 1 baking board, 20 wooden caps, 14 tins, 3 tarrins, 1 tin cover, 3 tin ladles, 30 tin spoons, 2 small boilers, 1 tea kettle, 6 lamps, 1 brass candlestick, 3 stressing irons, 1 spirtle, 1 crane, 1 pair tongs, 3 pokers, 2 shovels, 1 kitchen grate,

Abstract of the Treasurer's Intromissions,

RECEIPTS.

	£	s.	d.
Subscriptions	410	9	6
Donations	15	0	0
Legacies	19	12	5
Interest from Investments	434	4	1
James Guthrie Davidson's Bequest	38	1	6
Miss Peacock's Bequest	2	9	0
Miss Harris's Endowment—Amount unexpended	25	0	0
Miss Graham's Bequest	43	15	0
	£988	11	7
Deficiency	55	5	4
	£1043	16	11

EXTRAORDINARY RECEIPTS.

	£	s.	d.
LEGACIES—Thomas Blyth, Merchant	180	0	0
T. Weston Miln, Do.	20	0	0
Peter Rattray, Slater	45	0	0
James Guthrie of Craigie	100	0	0
Alex. Drummond, Powgavie	19	19	0
	£364	19	0
DONATIONS—The Trustees of the late Miss Graham of Kincaldrum	2000	0	0
Patrick Arnot, Blackness Terrace	25	0	0
Carried to Capital Account	£2389	19	0

EXPENDITURE.

	£	s.	d.
Clothes	141	13	1
Shoes	45	0	11
Groceries	77	17	11
Bread	60	16	11
Butcher Meat	82	10	10
Meal and Barley	63	4	0
Milk	46	6	6
Potatoes and Vegetables	16	17	3
Coals, Gas, and Water	66	0	6
Incidental House Expenses	17	11	1
	£617	18	2
Salaries—Master and Matron	200	0	0
Physician	5	5	0
Secretary	20	0	0
Treasurer	20	0	0
Servants' Wages and Music Teacher	47	0	0
	£292	5	0
Annuity payable under Miln's Bequest	5	0	0
Feu Duty and Fire Insurance	7	11	9
Taxes	10	16	0
Stationery, Printing, Books, &c.	20	16	4
Repairs and Improvements	37	9	4
House Furnishings	18	9	9
Ironmongery	10	7	9
Miscellaneous Expenses	23	6	7
Deficiency of 1873-74—Brought forward	425	7	6
	£1043	5	8
	0	11	3
	£1043	16	11

JOHN MILN, *Treasurer.*

. . . and found correct.

ROBT. R. RITCHIE, *Auditor.*

2 kitchen tables, 2 chairs, 1 pair bellows, 2 brooms, 1 whitening brush, 6 washing tubs, 2 water buckets, 1 pig trough, 2 tin basons, 1 scrubbing brush, 1 bread toaster, 1 salt backet, 1 small wooden cog, 1 coal scuttle, 2 large boilers, 1 white iron can, 1 small flagon, 2 steam pipes, 3 wooden rollers, 4 table knives, 3 forks, 3 bells, 3 bedroom grates, 2 fenders, 1 set fire irons.

•Mistresses Schoolroom
1 desk and stool, 1 large and 5 small tables, 10 large and 7 small forms, 3 water casks.

•Bedrooms
1 portrait of Doctor Bell, 3 tent beds with check curtains, 1 mahogany table, 11 small and 2 elbow chairs, 1 large wardrobe, 17 bed frames, 1 eight day clock, 1 hatchet, 2 orphan boxes with keys.

•Master's Schoolroom
1 desk and stool, 5 tables, 21 forms, 10 new bibles, 2 volumes of teachers assistant, 1 copy Scotts lessons, 12 silver medals, 2 quarters quills, 15 copies New Testament, 1 new school bell, Christ's Sermon 37 copies, Christ's Miricales 45 copies, History of Our Saviour 26 copies, Christ's Discourses 15 copies, National Society School Books 5 copies, Catechal Instruction 3 copies, abridged history of the bible 4 copies, Introductions to Christian Religion 2 copies, Lectures on Church Catichism 5 copies, Dutys of the Sick 8 copies, Horslys sermons 28 copies, 15 quire foolscap paper.

Why were the children at the Orphanage?

The early records of the Dundee Orphan Institution reveal hundreds of stories of family tragedy. These records provide information about a child's name, date of birth, previous address and who had submitted the request that they be admitted, as well as details about the child's parents, including date and cause of death and the father's occupation.

Research by The Friends of Dundee Archives found that children became residents of the Orphanage for many reasons.

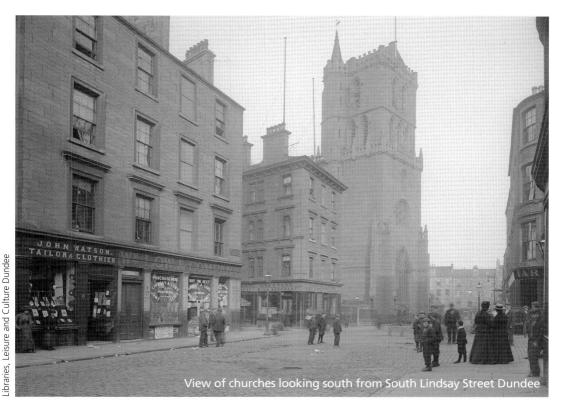

View of churches looking south from South Lindsay Street Dundee

Perhaps both parents had died, their mother had died during or soon after childbirth, or, after years of struggle, a surviving parent was unable to look after any of their children or had to hand a couple of their offspring to the Orphanage in the hope that their other children would survive, or perhaps an unknown father had left behind a woman with no means to live and an extra mouth to feed.

One record noted: 'The girl was very destitute when admitted about two years ago. Her father was then unable to follow his occupation as a weaver and now having been found dead, she is completely destitute.'

Violent deaths and risky occupations such as seafaring accounted for a few of the orphaned children. A girl who was admitted to the Orphanage in 1838 had lost her father when The Forfarshire sank off the Northumberland coast, the shipwreck which catapulted lighthouse keeper's daughter Grace Darling into the Victorian media spotlight.

Disease rather than accident, misfortune or murder claimed most of the orphans' parents, with consumption proving the most deadly of all. In the first 50 years, 60% of the orphans had lost one or both parents to tuberculosis. In addition, the Friends of Dundee City Archives pointed out, the surprisingly high proportion of orphans whose fathers were shop workers highlights the poor conditions the city's shoemakers, tailors and watchmakers lived and worked in.

'The striking feature is that these were not the idle and workshy but simple folk who, in a hard and unremitting environment, experienced serious illness or gross misfortune,' wrote the researcher. 'The margin for survival was precariously slim.'

Leaving The Orphanage

The 1821-1911 Admissions Register for Dundee Orphan Institution, which is held by The City of Dundee Archives, provides a glimpse of what happened to the orphans after they left, usually about the age of 14.

Many of the boys became apprentices in Dundee's booming manufacturing and weaving industries, and, at least in the early days of the Orphanage, a significant proportion went to sea. However, the Admissions Register shows that they also became bakers, mechanics, ironmongers, clerks and blacksmiths – and one was apprenticed to a dentist in South Tay Street while another found a job in the relatively new printing industry as a compositor.

Alexander Neilson, who was born in Montrose in 1851, was apprenticed to a local grocer for the sum of four shillings a month. However, it appears a shopkeeper's life wasn't for Alex as he 'went to sea and was drowned, 1872'.

The girls of the Orphanage had a very restricted career choice: domestic service, looking after a sibling's children or, occasionally, learning a trade such as weaving or dressmaking. Admitted to the Orphanage at the age of ten, in 1873, Barbara Gabriel 'went to reside with her grandmother and to learn the steam looms', only to die of consumption in 1883, at the age of 26.

Margaret Smith was admitted to the Orphanage in 1826 following the death of her parents in Jamaica. Five years later, she became a servant to a tailor in Dundee's Overgate, although the records reveal that she left this post a few months later 'through the improper interferences of some relatives'.

Towards the end of the 19th century, there were more careers open for girls and the Orphanage's female residents were quick to take advantage of their new options. In 1867, one girl started training as a milliner while several were sent to 'learn the sewing machines' at a local leather merchants. Tailoresses, cloak makers and Pupil Teachers all appear in the register, with some of the girls finding employment in the Orphanage and others getting married.

Very occasionally, the records show children being 'rediscovered' by their family or adopted. One girl was adopted by a seemingly unknown American family and went to live with them in Maine, while several were provided with a passage to America by relatives living there and set off on their own to a new life on the opposite side of the Atlantic.

Occasionally, orphans fell into bad ways. George Craigie was expelled in 1854 for theft and reset. And, although conditions at the Orphanage would have been better than trying to survive alone in Dundee's slums, some children refused to adhere to the strict rules and regulations and there are regular reports of children leaving 'without sanction', including Charles Stirling, who was admitted in January 1827 and ran off a month later.

A significant proportion of the boys went to sea

Photo courtesy of Dundee City Archives

There are many heartrending notes in the Admissions Register – 'died of consumption' and 'drowned' are written across many entries. Seven-year-old James Andrew was admitted to the Orphanage in December 1858 only to die of consumption soon afterwards. Alongside his record is the touching note, 'Buried by his friends'.

Hugh Tait was the son of a seaman who had been lost at sea and was admitted to the Orphanage in 1835 following the death of his mother. Hugh left the Orphanage to be an apprentice in one of Dundee' shipbuilding yards but the lure of the sea proved too strong. Several years later, Hugh met the same fate as his father.

Chapter 4

A New Home For Dundee Royal Orphan Institution

On September 29, 1870, Dundee Royal Orphan Institution's new home, Carolina House, was formally opened and 55 children moved into the new building, which was also a school for the orphans.

Built on 'a most amenable site' on the south side of Craigie Terrace, with views across the Tay, The Dundee Courier & Argus described Carolina House as a 'villa'.

'The building is on three storeys and contains large and airy dormitories, classrooms, sewing rooms, dining hall, kitchen and scullery, wash house and laundry, lavatories, bathrooms etc besides the apartments occupied by the Master and Matron,' continued the newspaper article. 'There are spacious grounds surrounding the building and there is plenty of room for the children amusing themselves.'

The Directors' Reports for the next few years show that the children and staff settled in well at their new abode, with each report outlining the numbers of children in residence (usually about 55) and the various trades the boys went to when they left, with, at this time, the girls almost always going into domestic service.

However, towards the end of the 19th century, the Directors of Dundee Royal Orphan Institution decided steps should be officially taken to support orphans when they left Carolina House. An After Care Fund was established, which helped former pupils maintain themselves while they were looking for work or undertaking apprenticeships.

The Directors' Report of 1889 shows that 71 children had resided there over the previous 12 months. 'In the course of the past year,' the report states, 'one of the children died of heart disease and sixteen others who have completed their term have left the Institution. Of the boys, two have gone abroad and the others to learn various handicrafts. The girls have all gone to domestic service.'

The Directors' Reports also provide information about days out and special events at the Orphanage. One annual treat was a visit to DM Brown's department store for the DM Brown Tea Party and the children would regularly enjoy trips to the countryside – often to Pitmuies, near Guthrie, jaunts 'up the river' or to the beach at Arbroath.

There also appears to have been a programme of talks. In November 1897, Dr Peter Rattray, who had tended to Mary Slessor during one of her illnesses and was a well-known benefactor to many Dundee charities, gave a talk to the children at the Orphanage about his travels in Central Africa.

Occasions such as Christmas were possibly celebrated more in the Orphanage than in the homes of most working class families at the end of the 19th century. In 1897, the Dundee Courier began a report on that year's Christmas party with a quote: 'This place is wrongly

D.M. Brown's department store was established in 1888

Girls were taught skills such as knitting from a young age

named,' remarked a lad at the Orphanage. 'It really isn't an orphan institution at all.'

The article went on to describe how: 'Sixty bright faced boys and girls were made the recipients of toys and dolls and sweets and crackers, which certainly did not inspire one with the usual feeling of pity that the word 'orphan' calls out.'

Another highlight of the year was the annual Reunion Day, which crowds of people flocked to. This was a chance for former residents to meet up and also say thank you to the staff for improving their start in life but it was also a way of showing the many benefactors and fundraisers who helped the Orphanage survive just what their money was doing.

There would be exhibitions showcasing the high standards of the girls' embroidery, knitting and needlework, as well as the chance to try some of the dishes they had cooked, while the boys showed off their woodworking skills. This would be followed by demonstrations in the gym of 'fan drill, Indian clubs and dumbbells' by the girls while the boys demonstrated their gymnastic skills on the rings, parallel and horizontal bars.

'These were watched by the ladies with mingled wonder and admiration,' reported The Courier in 1903, 'which intensified when Mr Lindsay, the gymnastics instructor, gave a marvellous exhibition on the horizontal bar.'

Centenary Celebrations of Dundee Royal Orphan Institution

The Centenary

The centenary of Dundee Royal Orphan Institution was marked on June 9, 1915 by a function at the Orphanage. This was attended by a 'large gathering of friends and well-wishers', which included a long list of ex-Provosts, local aristocracy, clergy, mill owners and ship owners – not unlike those who had attended the early meetings of the Society which founded the Orphanage. Unfortunately, due to the outbreak of World War 1, many of those who had benefitted from the services provided by the Orphanage were unable to attend but the orphans who were resident at the time sang hymns and a former resident, who had travelled from Calcutta, unveiled one of eight commemorative glass windows, now lost, which had been paid for by ex-residents and pupils.

In honour of the occasion, the Master, Mr TM Davidson, wrote a touching open letter to the children who had been at Dundee Orphanage during the 22 years he held the post of Master, with his wife as Matron.

'This letter is written especially for you, our dear children, whom we have 'spanked' and loved for twenty two years. In most cases the memory of the spanking has gone and that of the love remains. Many of you we have not seen since you left for one or other of the Colonies but the Directors have a care for the boys and girls who have left and there is always a bed, a meal and a welcome for you.

'I would like to say something about Children I have met – our soldiers and sailors, our girls, our dead, our two Little Nells, Daddy's girl, the boy who turned on all the water taps the first day he was in the house, the boy who cut off 28 buttons to play 'mites' and as a punishment had to sew them all on again…

'You had a lot of work but you had lots of fun. You remember 'the cuddie', 'the Captain and the band', 'The Ghost' (the boy who should have been frightened but was not is now a lieutenant), 'the chamois strap', 'The Brussel sprouts', 'Roddie and the hens' and the 101 things to which we were conveniently blind and deaf!'

Messages sent by former residents on the Centenary

"Many thanks for the book of songs you sent us. Glad to hear so many of our boys are serving with the colours. We would be glad to take our places alongside of them. We may get the chance before the war is over."
• *DH and JR (apprentices, SS Barn Cawdor, Bombay)*

"I have now built my own house – six rooms and a bathroom in birch. Bad trade started when I began my house but you taught us pluck at the Orphanage and I went right ahead."
• *AB, Vermont, USA*

"I should like to be at home for the centenary. What a grand reunion that will be. I am always glad to see any sailor boys from the Orphanage when they come here. It is a pleasure to show them round."
• *PB, Melbourne*

"You will be wondering who the wedding cake is from and who Mrs C is. Well, it is from your old pupil, JM. I have a good husband and we are very happy. One day, we hope to visit the Home which made a girl fit to fight the temptations of life."
• *JM / Mrs C, Montreal*

"I met one of the former pupils the other day and what a lot we had to talk about. It is only after we have seen a little of the world that we realise how much we were sheltered and cared for in the dear Old Home."
• *AC, Edinburgh*

Case Study – Sandy Anderson

Several years ago, as part of research for a feature about Carolina House for www.angusheritage.com and which later appeared in The Scots Magazine, I met Bill Pollock from Staffordshire, who had recently discovered that his grandfather was brought up in Dundee Royal Orphan Institution.

"My grandfather, Alexander 'Sandy' Anderson, was admitted to the Dundee Orphanage in 1875," Bill told me.

"My great-grandparents, Thomas and Mary Anderson, had moved from Dundee to South Shields in Durham following the birth of their second son. Three years later, in 1866, my grandpa, Sandy Anderson, was born but, for some unknown reason, by the time of the 1871 Census, five-year-old Sandy was living with his maternal grandmother in Dundee.

"In June 1873, Sandy's mother died of TB, followed later that year by his father. Sandy remained in Dundee and, when his grandmother died in 1875, he was sent to the Orphanage.

"During his time there, Sandy received sporadic visits from his brother Tom, who, like his father, was a plasterer. On leaving the Orphanage, Sandy was engaged by a Dundee firm as a clerk before moving back to South Shields and joining his brother in the plastering trade. In 1895, my grandfather married Barbara Blakiston and they had three sons and five daughters, including my mother.

"Grandfather Sandy came to live with us in 1957, when he was 91, and he died a fortnight short of his 92nd birthday."

Education

For 80 years, Dundee Royal Orphan Institution not only provided an education to the children who lived there but also to the many children who attended as day pupils, often before they went to start their shift in the mills.

However, in 1895, it was decided that, to reduce the constant financial pressure, educating day pupils would cease and most of the children who lived in the Orphanage would attend local primary schools, such as Glebelands. Several of the orphans won bursaries and scholarships and attended Morgan Academy and Dundee High School, which were both fee-paying establishments, where a high proportion (although only three girls) were awarded dux medals and school prizes.

'Experience has proved that the policy of sending the older pupils to schools outside has been a very beneficial one,' wrote one of the Directors in 1915. 'It affords a better preparation for the discipline of life which awaits the children than if they were brought up solely in an institution.'

A fairly major change occurred in 1918, when the education of the children in the Orphanage became the responsibility of the local authority. As a result, most of the children started attending local primary schools and although a number continued to be schooled at Dundee Royal Orphan Institution, this practice ceased in 1953.

World War 1

It was a matter of great pride at the Orphanage that 51 former pupils signed up to fight in World War 1. The fact that they were all accepted for active service illustrates the high standards of health and nutrition at Carolina House. In 1914, 40% of volunteers were rejected for medical reasons, often on account of malnutrition.

Of the 51 who signed up, 12 were killed in action. One former pupil, John H Smith, died of his wounds after the retreat from Mons. "The discipline of the army changed a somewhat wild boy into an earnest, industrious man," recalled Mr TM Davidson, Master of the Orphanage while John Smith was a resident. "He visited the house seven times before mobilisation."

• On January 15, 1919, a memorial plaque was erected to the 12 ex-residents who had been killed in action.

Private	George	Buchanan	RFA
Eng Lt	Thos	P Brodie	Australian Forces
AB	James	Christie	RHVR
Private	Gilbert	Mathers	RSF
Sergeant	John	McKenzie	1st Black Watch
Sergeant	Thomas	Philip	Canadian Forces
2nd Officer	James	Robertson	Merchant Marine
Private	John	Scott	Australian Forces
AB	Charles	Sharp	RHVR
Private	Duncan	Smith	Canadian Forces
Sergeant	John	H Smith	1st Black Watch
Trooper	William	Wood	MM Innis Dragoons

After the war, DC Thomson, head of the publishing company which ensured Dundee will forever be known for journalism as well as jute and jam, made a substantial donation of £1000 to the Orphanage in memory of his only son Conrad, who lost his life in 1918, at the age of 14. Conrad, who was at Fettes College in Edinburgh, developed peritonitis and as all the top surgeons were away in the Great War, he was unable to be saved.

During World War 1 the home was used as a temporary base for officers from The Royal Navy Air Service. The Orphanages Centenary booklet states; "on the mantelpiece has been placed a unique timepiece, the gift of the officers and men of the Royal Naval Air Service as a souvenir of their stay in the Orphanage from September to December last year. The timepiece, handed over by Major Gordon has been set in the boss of the propeller of Hydroplane 79 which was wrecked in St Andrews Bay on 1st Jan 1915."

Carolina House was designed by William Chalmers, believed to be the nephew of James Chalmers

Chapter 5

1920s and 1930s

The Twenties may well have been roaring in other places but in Dundee Royal Orphan Institution, life continued much as it had before. Orphaned children were cared for and educated until they were old enough to find a job, an apprenticeship or a position in a household and, as always, money was tight.

After researching the history of Carolina House, in 2008, staff member Brenda E McGilliard wrote: 'In the years that followed the end of the First World War, the notion of 'charity' changed radically. The importance of a balanced diet and less restricted home life meant that life was similar to a well-run boarding school.'

Until 1925, Mr TM Davidson was at the helm of this well-run organisation. Mr TM Davidson had previously been a teacher at Dundee High School and had taken up the post of Master, with his wife as Matron, in 1893. The couple were popular with staff and children and he was described as being a man of great piety, culture and humour – but also 'a born teacher, he drew the best from them.'

When his wife died in 1923, Mr Davidson was granted leave of absence and went to Australia, where he wrote a book called 'Stories Of My Bairns'. However, his collection of warm and caring tales of the children he'd encountered during his time at Dundee Orphan Institution only surfaced after his death, following a tragic accident, in 1925.

In his last will and testament, Mr Davidson left a note to his friends asking them to publish his stories – and a copy of this book is now one of the most treasured items of one of the men at the helm of Carolina House today, Stephen Clark.

A group photograph taken at the Orphanage

In 1928, the Directors recognised that times were changing with regard to children's welfare but they also realised that there would always be a need for an institution where children who had lost one or two parents or had been neglected or were from broken homes could be cared for. They successfully applied for a new charter, which enabled Dundee Royal Orphan Institution to provide accommodation to children in need from Angus, Fife and Perth – previously, due to the terms of the Royal Charter, they had only been allowed to provide care to children born in Dundee.

As the Great Depression of the 1930s hit home, it became increasingly difficult for boys at Carolina House to find work or apprenticeships. In 1938, an application from the British Overseas League for a boy to go to Australia was considered and a 12-year-old boy was identified as being ideal for this post. There is no record of him emigrating but three months later, two brothers went to British Columbia following another application from the British Overseas League.

Case Study 1 – George

George was the youngest of three who were brought to the Orphan Home. A terrible tragedy had taken place at their home. The father, a painter to trade, had dropped down dead at his work; a baby had been born that week and when the father's body was brought home, the shock killed the mother and the baby died, too.

Little George was taken to the funeral and saw his father, mother and baby brother put into the lap of mother earth.

For a few days after coming to us, George scarcely spoke to anyone. He went about like one in a dream. One evening, it was reported to me he took bread from the table instead of finishing his meal there, as the other boys did.

One evening, a special treat was given to the children and the tea table was laden with jelly-pieces, cookies and buns. George was spotted carrying away a jelly-piece and a bun from the table and going directly to the playground. There, in a corner, he dug a hole and placed the food in the ground, covering it carefully with earth.

Two boys approached him and said Matron would be angry with him for spoiling good bread. 'I'm no spoilin' bread,' George replied. 'I'm sendin' food to my mother!'

The boys told the story to Matron, who sent for George. 'Are you angry, Ma?' George sobbed.

'No George. You are a very unselfish boy to think about your mother and be willing to give her your nice piece but your mother is now in Happy Land and will never be hungry again. She will be pleased if you will just eat your piece yourself.'

The boy dried his tears, said 'Thank you, Ma' and from that day he became a much happier boy.
Abridged from TM Davidson's 'Stories Of My Bairns'

Case Study 2 – Leonard Robb

"I was born in 1928 and admitted to the Orphanage with my older brother, Terry, when I was seven years old. My father was already dead and my mother died soon afterwards.

"On our first day, we were kitted out with brand new clothes and then taken to another shop, where we were bought shoes, gym shoes, new Sunday shoes, Wellington boots and football boots.

"Breakfast was porridge and a roll and a cup of tea for the youngest, two rolls and a cup of tea for the older boys. We came back from school – Glebelands Primary and then Stobswell Secondary – at lunchtime and on Sunday, we went en-masse to St Matthews in Ferry Road.

"There were 30 boys and 30 girls in the Orphanage and each boy had a girl designated to darn his socks! Once a week, the boys all had to kneel at the dining table, take their shoes off and have their socks examined for holes."

Based on an interview with a Carolina House staff member

Cleaning shoes was one of the children's tasks

Chapter 6

World War II

With war on the horizon, in January 1939, the Directors of the Orphanage agreed on an evacuation plan.

In the event of war being announced, the pupils would be moved from the home, which was in close vicinity to Dundee Docks, an undoubted target for enemy fire, to the relative safety of Gray House in Invergowrie.

Following the announcement that Britain was at war with Germany, in September 1939, 62 children moved to the Orphanage's temporary country home, with schooling provided at the nearby villages of Liff, Logie and Invergowrie.

The Orphanage's risky position on the banks of the Tay might have been a concern to the Directors but to the Admiralty, this was ideal. They requisitioned the building for the duration of the war, at the very reasonable rent of £250 a year, and orphans were replaced by submariners and WRENS.

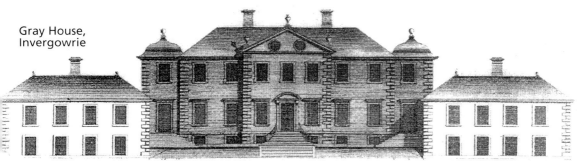

Gray House,
Invergowrie

Residents enjoying springtime

Although the children were very happy in their rural surroundings, the war triggered another financial crisis. With people's minds on loved ones fighting in foreign lands and seas, donations and subscriptions slumped to an all-time low of £60, which was barely enough to cover the Orphanage's annual bill for bread! In addition, the costs of the evacuation to Gray House had to be borne by the Orphanage rather than the Government, as the Directors had hoped.

To help out, the children picked potatoes on nearby farms, donating their wages of 5 shillings a day to the Orphanage – in 1945, the children donated a total of £24 and 5/-.

"As well as going to the tatties, we helped the local famers with other tasks, too," former pupil Leonard Robb revealed. "We used to make wee bunches of wheat into stooks and build them into pyramids, muck out the stables and, using cudgels we were given by the farmers, kill rats in the steading."

Despite war and straitened financial circumstances, the Orphanage continued its custom of taking the children on regular days out and, once a year, on holiday. The Evening Telegraph of October 22, 1941, reported that the children had been away for a month's holiday and the staff for three weeks. 'The children at Gray House are living in pleasant surroundings in the country,' the report concluded.

However, there was a tragic accident at Gray House towards the end of the war. A young boy, William Sellers, who was trying to sneak across the parapet of the roof from the boys' dorm to the girls' dorm, slipped and fell to his death on the gravel below.

In August 1946, the children and staff returned to the Orphanage on Ferry Road, where they were joined by several new children, who had lost their fathers during the war.

The Old Boys Lost At War

Fifty former pupils served their country in World War 2. Four were killed in action:

Peter Cant, Black Watch

James Grant, R.A.O.C

Albert Knowles, Black Watch

Victor Young, Royal Scots.

• On September 25, 1949, a plaque to the memory of these former pupils was unveiled at a ceremony at the Orphanage, which was attended by almost 80 people.

Case Study – Doug Thomson

"My father was a marine engineer whose ship was torpedoed in 1942. At that time, a merchant seaman's pay stopped there and then. My mother was left with four boisterous children aged from eight to two years and no money coming in. In 1946, she had to go into hospital and all four of us were sent to the Dundee Orphanage.

"The boy's play area had a football pitch on a cinder field. Boys were encouraged to play football and, in the summer, athletics. A concrete ramp led down from the entrance along the east wall. Boys would get inside ex-lorry tyres and be rolled down the slope to crash into the spiked railing at the bottom of the ramp!

"Occasionally, a few boys would climb over the spiked fence and into the tree-covered area leading down to the railway line. One boy got a spike from the railings in his knee. In summer, giant hogweed used to grow on the slopes. If the sap from the stems landed on the skin, this would cause blisters when exposed to the sun – and was one way of being found out for being 'out of bounds'.

"We were sometimes taken to see the circus when it was in town or films at the Broughty Ferry cinema. In particular, I remember Nicholas Nickleby – we really identified with the pupils in the school."
Abridged version of Doug's own memoire

Chapter 7

1947 – 1969

In literature and films, orphanages tend to be painted as harsh, uncaring places – but that definitely doesn't appear to be the case with Dundee Royal Orphan Institution. In 1947, the Lord Provost of Dundee went out of his way to praise the Orphanage's 'homely atmosphere' while letters sent by former residents to the Orphanage, and interviews, certainly appear to back this up.

"I loved my time there," said Sandra Taylor – who became a resident in 1956 when she was two years old. "It was brilliant. Every Christmas, we were invited to lots of Christmas parties, Santa Claus came to the Home and we got presents in a real jute sack. We went on holiday in the country – to Friockheim and Comrie – and were even taken to see The Beatles at The Caird Hall!"

After a slight decrease in the number of children being cared for, the Children's Act of 1948 – and the introduction of the Welfare State – triggered a rise in residents. By the start of the 1950s, 55 children were being cared for at Dundee Royal Orphan Institution.

To accommodate the larger numbers of children and thanks to a limited amount of state funding, in 1960, extensive improvements were made, including the addition of 'comfortable sitting room and cosy playroom'.

In 1950, a fundraising leaflet published by Dundee Royal Orphan Institution described how: 'Childhood here is bright, healthy and essentially happy… There are no locked gates, no feelings of restriction or restraint, no uniforms proclaiming the 'Institution child'. One newly admitted girl, when asked how she was getting along, replied 'Fine. I get plenty to eat and braw claes.'

'It is not for nothing that the men and women who have gone forth into the world from the Orphanage remember it not as 'The Home' but as 'Home'.'

In 1961, following a proposal regarding the running of children's homes in Dundee and, in particular, that Dundee Royal Orphan Institution be run by the local authority, a meeting was called between the Directors of the Orphanage and the Secretary of State. As a result, it was decided the Orphanage would remain in the hands of the Directors and supported by voluntary subscribers or benefactors – but the number of Directors would be reduced from seven to two and two co-opted Directors, from Dundee Council and Angus Council, would join the Board.

It was also decided that Dundee Royal Orphan Institution would change its name to Carolina House – the name the organisation carries to this day.

By then, the children staying there could no longer be referred to as 'orphans' as there were other reasons they needed to be provided with residential care. 'Many of the children come from homes broken by the tragedies of cruelty, divorce and sheer neglect,' explained Garnet Guthrie in a 1965 issue of The Scots Magazine.

'One girl was brought to the Home after being picked up off the street,' he wrote. 'She was the dirtiest, filthiest child ever admitted. Her clothing had to be burned and her infested hair shampooed and toothcombed. Scrubbed, then dressed in new clothes, she was stood before a long mirror. Before her was a bonny lass, with pink cheeks and gold-coloured hair. Slowly she passed her hand over her face and down over her new dress.

'Then she burst into tears. 'O', she wailed. 'That's no me!' Today, that child is one of the happiest and most helpful in the Home.'

Another major change was introduced by the new Board of Directors. Carolina House, its residents and staff were split into three family-group homes. Each 'home' consisted of eight to twelve residents, a Housemother and an assistant, with a supervisor in overall charge. "These units, it is hoped, will provide a family atmosphere, in place of the prevailing boarding school atmosphere," said TH Thoms, chair of the Directors, in 1965.

Orphanage Costs: Costs per head per annum

- 1815 - £9
- 1871 - £18
- 1915 - £27
- 1965 - £7 per head per week

Case Study 1 – Hazel Buick

"I remember good times and bad," Hazel Buick - who was admitted to the Orphanage in 1951 at the age of 5 - told Brenda E McGilliard. "There were fun times, having pillow fights and the like and we were always well-fed and clothed.

"There were 30 girls in three dorms – the wee dorm, the middle one then the older girls - while the oldest girls could move into the single room in the attic. There was a sewing room where we would sew, knit, embroider and darn socks. And the girls had to do the washing and ironing for everyone, using a mangle and a tin bath for blankets and sheets.

"At the time, I thought being brought up in an orphanage was normal. In fact, other kids at school were jealous because the orphans had new uniforms!"

Case Study 2 – Les Lumb

"I went to Carolina House in 1956, when I was 4. My mum had passed away and my dad found it difficult to look after the eight children left behind.

"I have so many memories of the Orphanage. We were very well cared for and there was always something going on – trips to the theatre, picnics, sport, Boys Brigade and lots of football.

"The Matrons were the backbone of the Orphanage. They showed all 60 of us a lot of love, patience and care, although they were strict. They worked so hard. They knitted and sewed for us, made sure there was food on the table for us and sometimes even told white lies so we didn't get the belt from the Superintendent.

"We used to get the belt – or a reduction in pocket money - for not eating our food, not taking the buttons out of shirts, coming home the wrong way from school, swearing, not cleaning teeth properly, destroying our shoes, poor homework, fighting, having the light on in the dormitory when we were supposed to be sleeping...

"But I've no regrets about my time in Carolina House. It taught me to stand on my own two feet and show respect to others.

"Those were happy times."

Les (left) with his brothers Stan and Alan (far right) entertaining OAPs with their group, The Hewdrops.

44

Chapter 8

1970 – 1995

Although, by the early 1970s, children living in Carolina House were more likely to be from broken homes rather than orphans, the organisation's ethos of providing as near a real home as possible to children and young people continued.

"There was a very happy feeling throughout the place," said the late Bill Christie, former Chair of the Board of Trustees and a member of Dundee Rotary Club, one of the Orphanage's staunchest supporters, providing financial assistance, taking the children on outings and arranging special events such as Christmas parties. "The children were well cared for and I'm very honoured to have been involved in the running of Carolina House."

From May 1970, in line with Government legislation, all children admitted to residential accommodation became the responsibility of the local authority. In 1981, for a variety of reasons, the local authority became dissatisfied with the service being provided by Carolina House and threatened an embargo – unless there was a marked improvement. "In December 1981, Bill Black was appointed Executive Director of Carolina House Trust and that was the beginning of a very innovative time there," recalls Angie MacDonald, who was a residential care worker/assistant manager at Carolina House Trust from 1982 – 2002.

"A good quality of care had always been provided at Carolina House but after Bill joined the team, everything took a giant leap forward. Service provision, the professionalism of the staff and, most importantly, providing the children at Carolina House with their own

A visit to RAF Leuchars

© DC Thomson & Co. Ltd.

space, their own clothes and a say in what happened in the day to day running of their home."

However, by 1983, it was obvious that the Carolina House building was no longer able to meet the modern day demands of residential care. "It was built specifically as an orphanage and reflected the ideas of the last century," Bill Black told the Evening Telegraph. "Obviously, ideas have changed since then and we need a place which would help rather than hinder our work."

This did not go down well with the residents of Carolina House, especially as they were angry that the Directors had announced the closure of Carolina House to the press without consulting staff or residents or considering other options. In fact, when they heard of plans to move out of the building they considered home, the young people set up an Action Committee, engaged the services of a solicitor to oppose the closure and collected 18000 signatures on a petition – to no avail.

With an ever-increasing need to provide residential care to children and young people with complex needs, the building was no longer fit for purpose. "The past ten to fifteen years have seen a greater emphasis on fostering and this has resulted in fewer children requiring residential care," wrote Bill Black.

"This is obviously an excellent focus but it is one of the factors forcing a shift of emphasis in the area of residential care. Today, children's homes have a greater number of children with behavioural problems and, for a variety of reasons, there would appear to be a number of older children coming into care. This, again, requires careful thought when planning a residential home's focus,"

In 1983, following the £180,000 conversion of Haring House at 281 Strathmore Avenue, Carolina House moved to a new facility. This had been specifically designed to provide residential to care for 22 young people, aged from 10 to 18 but mainly in the 14 to18 age group.

There were three units in Carolina House Trust's Strathmore Avenue facility: Scott House, Ogilvie House and Barrie House. The residents were closely involved in the décor and furnishing of their new home and were responsible for the names of the Houses remaining the same as they were at the original Carolina House.

The units were largely independent, with each one supervised by a team of four care staff and one part time domestic, under the direction of a team leader. The staff worked a shift rota which allowed for one team member to do 'sleep-in' duty, providing cover 24 hours a day, seven days a week.

"All our children have, in some way or another, suffered badly in their young lives," said Bill Black, who explained in an article in the Evening Telegraph that each child had a named member of staff who was responsible for their care. "Our children find it very difficult to trust other people and having one person, whom they know is interested in them, who cares about them, faults and all, goes a long way to establishing that vital bond of trust."

The concept of each child having a 'special' member of staff was highly innovative at the time and was an attempt to reduce the number of people residents had to relate to, while also clearly placing responsibility on the staff member concerned.

"Among the duties of the 'special' staff member is the supervision of the young person's general welfare – i.e. the management of the clothing budget, liaison with outside agencies (doctor, dentists, school/work, social workers etc) and the development of a relationship which would enable the young person to work through difficulties and develop appropriate social and practical skills," Bill wrote in a 1987 report. "No staff member should have more than two or, in special circumstances, three children allocated to them."

Scott House and Ogilvie House were residential units for children and young people, with Scott House being the unit for the younger children. Most of the study/bedrooms were shared by two residents, although some had a room to themselves, and each house had a kitchen, dining area, sitting room and laundry, while the recreation room and interview rooms were shared by all.

Unlike at the previous facility, the young people were expected to help with cooking and household tasks and each House had a weekly budget allocation for food, pocket money and incidental expenses.

A day trip to Glamis Castle

A friendly visit from the local constabulary

"This helped them to grow up with an awareness of the importance of budgeting and also taught them vital household skills, which had been impossible in the old building, with its industrial kitchen and laundry," said Angie MacDonald. "Working with their 'special' team member, they were involved in planning menus, cooking, doing the dishes, washing and ironing their clothes."

In another article in the Evening Telegraph in 1985, Bill Black stressed that the emphasis was on helping young people learn the life skills they would need when they left the care of Carolina House Trust. "Our aim is to establish, as near as possible, a normal family routine," Bill said.

Heather White was a member of Carolina House's residential care team. "When I first started working at Carolina House Trust, a young girl who stayed at Ogilvie House with her baby benefitted from the support provided," explained Heather.

"Over the period of time I was at the Strathmore Avenue facility, three girls with babies stayed there," added Angie McDonald. "This was groundbreaking and the staff were very involved in supporting the girls through pregnancy, birth and caring for the babies. By the time their babies were a year old, the girls had all moved to independent accommodation, with very positive outcomes."

Carolina House's longstanding policy of providing the children and young people in its care with holiday and trips continued. "When I was working there, we went on holidays to Butlins, the Isle of Wight, Torquay, a caravan in Wales, France and Spain," recalled Angie MacDonald. "The children would often decide where we were going and, when we were away, the budget was their responsibility – we'd regularly go without puddings for the week so we could have tea out one night.

"Carolina House also had a holiday home in Kingsbarns, which had been gifted to the Trust by a member of the Board, and we had access to a cottage on Balmoral Estate," continued Angie. "We'd take young people there so they could experience life away from the city, out of doors and miles away from whatever had happened or was happening in their lives. Going to the cottage was often a good way of managing difficult behaviour or getting to the root of a problem."

Angie explained that these trips were often funded by donations or the fundraising efforts of staff and residents. "One of our regular benefactors was an oil rig - Sedneth 701. The men on the rig were very generous and thanks to their donations, we were able to buy things we couldn't with the basic funds we received from the local authority, such as TVs and hi-fis and of course, holidays."

Barrie House was for young people who were preparing for independent living. It had seven single bedrooms and the emphasis was on preparing young people for leaving care. At Barrie House, young people could experience a taste of independence but with 24-hour support available from the team.

Another innovation introduced by Bill Black was the House Committee, which consisted of staff members, delegated Board members, Social Work and Child Guidance Service representatives and the consultant psychiatrist from Dundee Royal Infirmary, who latterly was based at Dudhope Young Persons' Unit. "This committee provided a much-needed bridge between staff and the Board," said Angie MacDonald. "In addition, having a psychiatrist on the committee was groundbreaking - and incredibly helpful, especially when discussing children's behaviour."

The committee met once a month and, as well as highlighting individual challenges faced by residents, enabled the Trust to consider how to deal with an issue that arose time and time again - the problems faced by young people when leaving residential care.

Visiting entertainment was a regular occurrence at the home

"This is an area of great concern," wrote Bill Black. "Young people leaving care experience greater difficulties in their search for independence than young people seeking independence from the relative security of a stable home and family environment."

It was only too apparent that a lot of ex-residents were struggling when they left the care of Carolina House Trust. "They kept returning, looking for help and guidance," said Doug Millar, who worked in Ogilvie House.

The main issues these young people were facing were:
• Finding a place to live
• Loneliness
• Lack of employment opportunities

As a result, the Carolina House Outreach Project was set up in 1987. This initiative involved a team of five workers providing 24 hour support, seven days a week and initially provided support to young people aged 15-18 years who had been residents of Carolina House. Later, this expanded to cover young people between the age of 15 and

25 who were in transition between residential, foster and mainstay care, or involved with the Social Work Department or independent living services within the City of Dundee.

Following negotiations with a housing association, Carolina House rented three flats in the Fintry area of the city and four older residents of Carolina House moved into these flats, with 24-hour on-call support, training programmes, group work, drop-in facilities, counselling and advocacy provided by the Outreach Project Team. "This was way ahead of its time and was very successful," said Angie MacDonald.

Two years later, the Carolina House Outreach Project had extended into a network of supported flats throughout Dundee, providing young people with a stepping stone and extensive support before moving into their own flat. Some of the young people who lived in these flats shared their homes with Community Service Volunteers, with the Outreach Project team always on call, while others were provided with 'sleep in' support by members of the Outreach Project team.

Doug Millar, who became a member of the Outreach Project team following his time at Ogilvie House, recalled that it was not uncommon to stop off at the local fish and chip shop for a late night supper to share with the young people. "You could have a blether and the young people would sometimes open up about what was going on in their lives," continued Doug. "But most of the time it was a cup of tea, a chat and a bit of telly."

The Outreach Project was based in Strathmore Avenue. Young people who lived in the supported flats, both ex-Carolina House residents and those referred by Dundee City Council, could visit for advice and support. In addition, there were various drop-in groups, including a group on a Wednesday night when young people and team members would cook a communal meal. "The Outreach Team experienced many happy and not so happy events with the young people," added Doug. "There was real sense of belonging for the young people. It was almost like an extended family".

The Outreach Project was very innovative for its time and organisations from across Scotland visited Carolina House Trust to research its success.

In 2001, Dundee City Council commissioned an outreach project supporting young people in their own flats and, in 2001, set up a joint Moving On Team (Throughcare and Aftercare) with Carolina House Trust. This arrangement continued until 2009.

Case Study 1 – Leah Henderson

"I'd been in various foster care homes which didn't work out when I went to Carolina House on the Ferry Road.

"I shared a bedroom with three other girls. We had a house mother, who we called Auntie, and it was part of my duties to look after the wee tots, bathing them and taking them to school.

"I was sent to foster parents in Fintry at one point but I wanted to return to the Home as, although it was strict, I was happy there. I think I'm a better person as a result of the time I spent there."

Carolina House Christmas party 1979

Carolina 1815 of Dundee

Chapter 9

1996 – 2015

In 1995, it was decided to close the residential units at Strathmore Avenue. The Trust moved to a new base at Roseangle in Dundee's West End, where it focused on providing innovative forms of care, such as the supported flats and outreach service, specialist training for staff and helping young people to develop the necessary skills to live in the community. In addition, the basement of the Roseangle building housed the Drop-In Clinic and was also the base for Carolina House Outreach Project.

In 1997, Carolina House Trust introduced its unique Care Rescue Service, which offered emergency residential care to young people in crisis, mainly as a result of the breakdown of their placement in foster care or residential care. This service covered 18 local authorities across the country.

"The Trust has been at the forefront of this area of work for many years," said Carolina House Trust Executive Director, Clive Wood, in 1995. "With the support of the community, we will continue with this invaluable work, providing education and care for vulnerable children – but within the context of 20th century thinking to meet the needs of today's young people."

The Trust also set up its Boat Project, which was established to provide young people with different experiences and opportunities. A fishing boat, Family's Pride, was borrowed for three years and renovated by volunteers. The boat was hired out and the funds raised enabled the Trust to take young people from all backgrounds to experience life at sea.

Tarvit Cottage

After the fishing boat was returned to its owner, a yacht, Carolina 1815, was bought, which was berthed on the west coast and used for the same purpose.

Carolina House Trust briefly moved back into residential care in 2000, when a large house was purchased in Fife to be used as a residential unit for very challenging young people. One year later, Tarvit Cottage, near Cupar, was purchased to extend the residential service (this cottage is still owned by the Trust and is rented to an organisation providing care for adults with learning difficulties). These units closed in 2011 following a change in local authority policy on residential care and a potential loss of funds.

In 2003, Carolina House Trust set up a foster care service for challenging young people, principally from the residential units in Fife. "This is now Carolina House Trust's principal activity and is expanding," said Stephen Clark of Carolina House Trust. "We deal with a wide range of young people but mostly those in long term or permanent foster care, offering placements to all local authorities but mostly to those from the east of Scotland.

"Foster care is about normalising young people's lives," continued Stephen. "It's about ensuring they feel safe and secure."

Carolina House Trust currently supports young people from Central Scotland, Fife,

Angus and Dundee who are in foster care. "We are a small organisation with fulltime foster carers and short term carers," said Stephen. "This enables us to be responsive – and personal."

And many of the traditions introduced over a century ago are still evident at Carolina House Trust with Christmas parties, outings and picnics all on the calendar.

The founding of the Orphan Society in 1815 was innovative for the time. It was one of the first charities dedicated to helping children in Scotland, and despite the fluctuating fortunes of the City of Discovery, the charity has remained committed to offering thousands of children the stable environment every young person deserves.

In 1997, the Trust's links with its orphanage past came to a very visible end when the original Carolina House on Ferry Road went on fire.

Plans to convert the building into a housing development appeared to go up in smoke as flames leapt through the roof of the Victorian orphanage. However, since then, the building has been restored and is now a complex of flats and houses.

The restored Carolina House, taken from Orphanage Bridge, Stannergate

Services Provided By Carolina House Trust in 2015

Foster Care

Foster care is the principal service provided by Carolina House Trust at the present time.

Carolina House Trust accepts referrals from across Scotland for foster care placements, which are principally offered in Angus, Dundee, Fife and Central Scotland and provide a number of different types of family-based care options.

These options include:

• **Emergency Placements** – This type of fostering involves caring for a young person or child who needs somewhere safe to stay immediately, usually for a few days.

• **Respite / Short Break Care** – Short break placements give parents or carers a break or offer additional support (all our full time foster carers receive paid respite, allowing them to take a break or go on holiday).

• **Short / Long Term Placements** – Short term foster carers provide a temporary place for a young person or child to live until they can return home to their family or move into a longer term fostering placement. This can last for a number of years or until the young person can move onto more independent living arrangements.

• **Permanent Placements** – This is a commitment to care for a child or young person into their adult life. These types of placement are used when a child or young person is deemed too old for adoption and involves looking after them until they are ready to live independently, after which contact and support would continue for as long as necessary. There can be a different legal basis to these placements, with foster carers sharing some of the parental rights which have been assumed by the local authority.

• **Parent and Child Placements** – This specialist foster care happens when a looked after young person becomes a parent and continues to live with their foster family. The foster carers provide support and guidance and help the young person to develop their parenting skills.

Foster care placements are supported by a team approach, which involves clear assessment of support needs, risks and personnel required to encourage positive outcomes. As Carolina House is more than a fostering agency, the organisation has access to a number of other professionals and resource workers with a wide range of skills, which can enhance foster care placement for a young person.

Throughcare and Aftercare Services

Throughcare and Aftercare Services for young people in Dundee are delivered through a partnership between Dundee City Council and Carolina House Trust, who have been working together with care leavers since 2003.

The local authority has statutory responsibilities to plan and prepare young people for leaving care, with legislation governing the type of service which should be provided, for example, providing advice, guidance and assistance to live independently.

Support Workers within the Throughcare and Aftercare Service provide one-on-one support with young people by helping them with budgeting and cooking skills, accessing work, training or education opportunities, as well as supporting young people to manage and furnish their own tenancy.

Children in foster care enjoy a visit to the fire station

In April 2015, extra support and greater rights for children and young people in care came into effect with the introduction of the Children and Young People (Scotland) Act 2014.

"These changes will be a challenge to local authorities and organisations such as Carolina House Trust," said Stephen Clark. "However, these changes will allow us to provide support for care leavers up to the age of 26, helping them move on to independent living at a pace which suits them."

Independent Reviewing Officer:

All young people who leave care are entitled to support from the local authority which is recorded as a Pathways Plan.

As part of the commissioned Throughcare and Aftercare services for Dundee City Council, Carolina House Trust employs an Independent Reviewing Officer. The officer's role is to review all Pathways Plans and to help the young people involved have a voice and ensure they have a support plan to meet their needs.

Supported Lodgings:

In 2010 Carolina House Trust was commissioned by Dundee City Council to set up a Supported Lodgings Service.

Supported Lodgings provide vulnerable and/or homeless young people who have been in care and are not ready to live independently with a safe, secure place to stay. Many care leavers have had a particularly difficult time in their earlier lives and therefore need various kinds of support to prepare for independent living.

Supported Lodgings Carers provide varying levels of practical and emotional support, with individuals and families providing young people with their own room and sharing their home with them. The aim of this service is to offer a protected, supportive environment which will enable young people to grow and develop the skills necessary for independent living.

The Supported Lodgings service is distinctive because it engages members of the local community to support and help vulnerable young people to live independently.

Supported Accommodation:

In October 2012, Carolina House Trust launched their Supported Accommodation Project, which is funded by The Big Lottery Fund.

"The Project works with the most vulnerable of care leavers to ensure successful life transitions from childhood to young adulthood when they leave the care system," explained Stephen Clark.

"Supported Accommodation achieves improved outcomes for these young people, who are likely to have had many moves within the care system, through providing individual, tailored packages of support, concentrating on areas such as work experience, training or further education, life skills and personal development.

"This support is provided step-by-step and at their pace as the young people are supported by staff in this crucial transitional period via a holistic, caring approach where they receive the support and level of care they require.

"Partnership working with a network of services including housing agencies, literacy projects and health services brings additional knowledge and skills, strengthening the project in meeting young people's needs and improving outcomes. Accommodation facilities with bedsits, flats and communal areas provide the safety, stability and nurturing this group needs to successfully move on to independent living."

Case Study 1 – Carolina House Trust Foster Carer: Andy Chalmers

Andy Chalmers has been a fulltime foster carer for Carolina House Trust for six years.

"I was previously a taxi driver, working nights, and when I was waiting at the taxi stance, I would often notice adverts on other taxis about becoming a foster carer and wonder if that might be something my partner, Caroline, and I could do," says Andy.

"Caroline and I had three young children, I was always very comfortable about being at home with the kids and looking after the day-to-day aspects of family life – and since my parents had moved out of our five bedroom house, we had a spare bedroom.

"Also, I'd been working on the taxis for too long and I knew I couldn't keep working long, anti-social hours with a young family. As a foster carer, I would be able to spend more time with my own kids while also helping other children.

"Caroline and I applied to Carolina House and after eight months of assessment and training, we were given our first placement, which was providing temporary foster care to a young girl with a lot of problems.

"Next came Jane*, who stayed with us for nearly five years and is still in regular contact with us, and then Susan*, who's been here for four years and is about to leave as she's going to college. Our latest placement, Ali*, has only been here for four months but she's also settled in really well.

"Most of the time, being a foster carer doesn't feel like a job. It is more challenging, however, when a child or young person first arrives.

"Jane* had a few issues to begin with, mainly because she wanted to stay with her dad and didn't want to go to school. She ran away a few times and had various run-ins with her social workers – until she realised the benefits of living in a settled home with a family. As a result, she turned the corner, stayed on at school until the end of sixth year and is now studying at college so she can become a social worker.

"For me, foster care is about opening your house and being as understanding as you can be, not being too rigid about rules and adapting to each child's needs."
*Names changed to protect individual identities.

Case Study 2 – Michelle

"Carolina House Trust has had a big impact on my life," explains Michelle (18), who was 16 and in an abusive relationship with an older man when she became pregnant.

"I'd been in local authority care from the age of 6 until I was 16 and once I left the home, I received support from Carolina House's After Care Service, which mainly involved one of their team members, Heather, helping me with independent living skills.

"As my baby's due date approached, the situation with my baby's father became even more serious but even though he was violent towards me, I had nowhere else to go.

"I was told that my baby would be removed at birth, which was the worst thing I could have heard. I'd been so excited about my baby's arrival but now, I didn't want him to come out.

"Then Heather asked my Throughcare Worker if she could give me and my baby somewhere safe to stay until I felt ready to cope on my own.

"After lots of meetings, it was agreed that Heather would become one of the Trust's Supported Lodgings Carers and I could stay with her for 12 weeks in a Supported Lodgings Placement. This would hopefully provide me with the support I needed to learn how to cope with my baby and also enable me to get away from the violent relationship I was in.

"So, two weeks before my baby was due, I was told I was going to stay with Heather and her family, under the care of Carolina House. That was the most amazing moment of my life.

"This was my chance. I was actually going to be able to take my baby home with me.
"After my son was born, we went home with Heather and she had decorated a room for us, which was so cute.

"It was really hard at the start as my plan had been to have our son and live happily ever after – but that was never going to happen.

"However, Heather was so good with me and my son and although I was meant to move into my own place after 12 weeks, at a meeting, I asked my Throughcare Resource Worker and my son's social worker if I could live with Heather and her family for another three months. I think that's when me and Heather really bonded.

"After a year, I moved into my own flat but we're still so close and see each other all the time. I consider Heather a mum and my son's gran, while her daughter and me feel like sisters. I've gained a family – and managed to cut out my ex from my life completely.

"I'm so grateful that the team at Carolina House gave me the chance. Without that, I don't know where I would be. They believed in me – and when someone believes in you, you start to believe in yourself.

"I'm now at college as I want to do social work so I can help other young people, I've got my own flat, I've got my friends back and I have my son, whose wee smile makes me feel amazing.

"Thank you, Carolina House. You've given me a family, my life and my beautiful son."

The Masters and Matrons at Dundee Royal Orphan Institution / Carolina House Trust

1815 - 1816	Mr David Adams & Miss Magdalene Moncur
1816 - 1821	Mr David Adams & Miss Hendry
1821 – 1844	Mr & Mrs Borland
1844 – 1853	Mr & Mrs Guild
1853 – 1855	Mr & Mrs Ross
1855 – 1858	Mr & Mrs Currie
1858 – 1893	Mr & Mrs Peddie
1893 – 1918	Mr & Mrs TM Davidson
1918 – 1935	Mr & Mrs James Davidson
1953 – 1976	Mr & Mrs DG Meldrum

Officer In Charge / Superintendent

1976 – 1979	Angus McDonald
1979 – 1981	George Walker

Executive Director, Carolina House Trust

1981 – 1994	Bill Black
1994 – 2007	Clive Wood

Director of Operations

2007 – 2015	Joyce Clark
2015	Stephen Clark (Acting Director of Operations)

Carolina House Trust Directors, 2015

David Gilbertson (Chairman of Board)
George Taylor (Deputy Chairman)
Robert Heywood
Donald Mackenzie
Gavin Strachan
Jill Shimi
Iain Symon
Nisbet Torrrance

65

The Orphanage Song

May all good luck attend our home
A long and bright career;
And may it prosper in God's sight
Through each successive year

Chorus
The orphanage, the orphanage,
Our childhood's happy home.
We'll ne'er forget the pleasant days
Wherever we may roam

But soon our days at home will end
And we shall then depart
To fight life's battle, long and hard,
With brave courageous heart.